A Pocket Guide to The

CARRIAGE ROADS

Of Acadia National Park

3rd Edition

A Pocket Guide to The

CARRIAGE ROADS

Of Acadia National Park

3rd Edition

FOR

HIKERS · BIKERS · JOGGERS
CROSS-COUNTRY SKIERS

BY **DIANA F. ABRELL**
MAPS BY **BUNNY LADOUCEUR**
PHOTOGRAPHY BY **SUE ANN HODGES**

With a New History of the Carriage Roads
BY **ANDREW VIETZE**

Down East

ACKNOWLEDGEMENTS

Since 1985, when *A Pocket Guide to the Carriage Roads* was first published, through the publication of this new expanded edition, I have received assistance and support from many individuals. The person, however, to whom I am most indebted is Bunny LaDouceur. Like me, Bunny loves the carriage roads and has spent many enjoyable hours wandering them. Bunny also possesses the talent and training to create accurate maps that are easy to follow. For this, as well as her enthusiastic and enduring loyalty to this project, I am truly grateful.

Others who have provided assistance, advice, support, and just plain hard labor include: Earl Brechlin, John Clark, Judy Hazen Connery, Dan Kane, Bob Rothe, Gary Stellpflug, Lois Winter, Karin Womer, and my family — Andrea, Leif, and Joe Abrell. Thanks so much.

ISBN: 978-0-89272-924-1

Camden, ME

CONTENTS

7   Introduction

9   How to Use This Book (with legend for all maps)

12   Carriage Road System Map

14   Rules

15   Courtesy and Safety

17   Eagle Lake Loop

19   Aunt Betty's Pond Loop

23   Witch Hole Pond Loop

27   Jordan-Bubble Ponds Loop

31   Jordan Stream Loop

35   Day Mountain Loop

39   Little Long Pond Loop

43   Redfield Hill Loop

47   Hadlock Brook Loop

51   Amphitheatre Loop

55   Giant Slide Loop

59   Around Mountain Loop

61   History by Andrew Vietze

71   Distance Index

Introduction

Mt. Desert Island is home to a truly unique scenic and recreational feature — its carriage roads. The 51-mile system of one-lane gravel roads and granite bridges combines the best in natural and manmade beauty, as the paths rise to spectacular ocean overlooks, traverse spruce- and hemlock-covered mountains, skirt glacier-formed lakes, and cross babbling brooks.

Responsible for the concept and the creation of the carriage roads was John D. Rockefeller, Jr. — multimillionaire, philanthropist, steward of natural resources, and a man ahead of his time. Rockefeller knew that the newly popular automobile could only distract from the grandeur and quietude of Mt. Desert Island's forests, mountains, and ponds. In 1913 he embarked on a 27-year project that would eventually include construction of 51 miles of roads, 17 bridges, and two gatehouses. Rockefeller employed local Maine engineers Charles P. Simpson, Paul D. Simpson, and Walters G. Hill to construct the roads and bridges. Noted architects William Welles Bosworth and Charles Stoughton designed most of the bridges, and the gatehouses were designed by the eminent architect Grosvenor Atterbury.

Working in concert with the National Park Service in the development of Acadia National Park, Rockefeller eventually presented the carriage road system, as well as a third of the land now within the park, as a gift to the people of the United States.

Maintained primarily by Rockefeller until 1960, the roads later fell into disrepair due to lack of funding. In 1989, a resource study on the carriage roads documented the sequence of the roads' development and construction and made recommendations for their rehabilitation and maintenance. In the 1990s and early 2000s, an $8 million rehabilitation program, paid for with federal and matching private funds, made possible rehabilitation of most of the NPS carriage roads and bridges. Funds raised by Friends of Acadia, a private nonprofit foundation, have provided a permanent endowment that enables continued rehabilitation and annual maintenance of the NPS portion of the system. Acadia National Park is partnering with Friends of Acadia in efforts to support this carriage road endowment fund.

The carriage roads, planned for horse-drawn carriages, are today enjoyed by joggers, hikers, bicyclists, cross-country skiers, horseback riders, and even an occasional horse-drawn carriage. Motorized vehicles are not allowed. For small children, the elderly, and the handicapped, the carriage roads are ideal, since the paths are smooth and follow natural contours with gradual rises.

The entire system lies on the eastern half of Mt. Desert Island on the coast of Maine. Forty-three of the 51 miles are within Acadian National Park; the rest are on private land but are open to the public.

How to Use This Book

The purpose of this guide is twofold. The first is to assist you in finding your way over the maze of carriage roads. A small plaque attached to each intersection signpost is keyed to an

intersection number, e.g. (16) on the loop maps in this book. As you approach intersections on the carriage roads, compare the number on the signpost to the numbers on the map to see where you are and which way you need to turn to complete your loop.

The second purpose is to make the carriage roads more useful to you by dividing them into twelve loops ranging from one to eleven miles in length. The cumulative distances (measured clockwise) around each loop are shown on the maps at each intersection and bridge. Joggers and cross-country skiers wanting to travel specified distances may find this distance information useful. The map in the center of the book shows the entire carriage road system and serves as an index to the individual loop maps. The legend printed below is a key to all the maps in the book.

Various wide foot trails and shortcuts intersect with the carriage roads and are often a source of confusion to carriage road users. These are shown on the maps by dashed lines. True carriage roads are usually about 16 feet wide and are often bordered by coping stones and drainage ditches.

- - - -	WIDE FOOT PATH OR GRAVEL ROAD		ACADIA NATIONAL PARK BOUNDARY
✗	HIGHEST ELEVATION	=	PAVED ROAD
↙	DIRECTION OF TRAVEL	▣	MARSH
☆	LOOP START & FINISH	⌒	STREAM
⌒	CARRIAGE ROAD	△	PEAK
14	INTERSECTION NUMBER	■	BRIDGE
—P	ACCESS TO PARKING	2.3	DISTANCE FROM START OF LOOP IN MILES

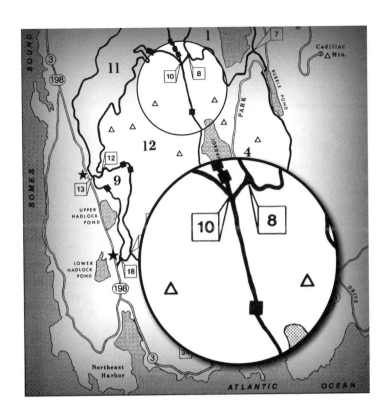

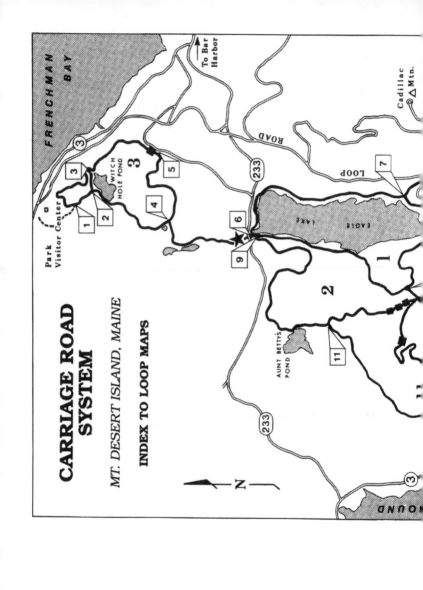

CARRIAGE ROAD SYSTEM

MT. DESERT ISLAND, MAINE

INDEX TO LOOP MAPS

N

FRENCHMAN BAY

To Bar Harbor

Cadillac △ Mtn.

Park Visitor Center

WITCH HOLE POND

EAGLE LAKE

AUNT BETTY'S POND

ROAD

LOOP

233

3

1

2

3

4

5

6

7

9

11

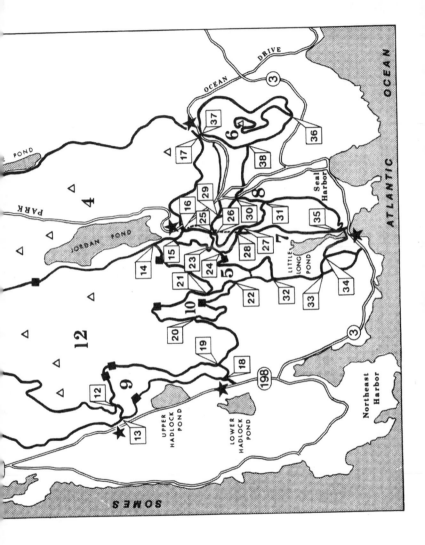

Rules

■ No motorized vehicles are allowed on the carriage roads.

■ Pets must be on leashes of six feet or less.

■ Horses are prohibited on the Witch Hole Pond and Eagle Lake loops, except between intersections 7 and 8.

■ Picnicking is allowed anywhere along the carriage roads, but fires and camping are prohibited.

■ Bicycles are prohibited on privately owned carriage roads outside the boundary of the national park as well as on hiking trails. Please respect posted regulations.

■ Swimming, wading, and pets are prohibited in public drinking water supplies. Please respect posted regulations at lakes and ponds.

Courtesy and Safety

Bicyclists should not ride at excessive speeds. The carriage roads are designed to provide an opportunity for gentle recreation and communion with nature for everyone. Stay to the right and pass on the left only after giving a clear warning.

Horses are unpredictable, powerful creatures and should be approached with caution. Bicyclists should prepare to stop and await instructions before passing horses and carriages, especially when passing from behind. Do not attempt to touch horses, as they may be easily startled.

Carry water at all times of the year when planning to go more than a mile or two. Dehydration occurs just as easily in cold weather as in warm.

Begin cross-country ski trips early in the day. It becomes dark by 4:30 p.m. between November and February. Cross-country skiers will appreciate the thoughtfulness of those who refrain from walking in ski tracks.

During the peak season, parking areas at popular carriage road loops are often completely filled. The resulting overflow parking along the paved roads can create potentially hazardous conditions for pedestrians. Please be cautious when walking between cars or crossing the road on foot.

Carriage roads are easily damaged in wet weather and may be closed briefly during the spring or at other times. Check ahead with park headquarters (207-288-3338).

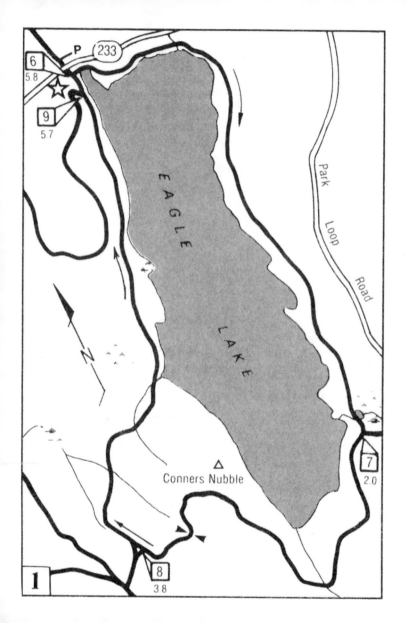

P (233)

6
5.8

9
5.7

EAGLE LAKE

Park Loop Road

N

△
Conners Nubble

7
2.0

8
3.8

1

1

Eagle Lake Loop

One of the most popular outings in Acadia National Park is the nearly six-mile loop around Eagle Lake. This loop is surfaced with fine gravel so that it is especially suitable for bicycles as well as wheelchairs and strollers. Horses are not allowed on this loop.

Park your car in the Eagle Lake parking area about three miles west of Bar Harbor on Rte. 233. Walk west along the foot trail to where you can turn left and go under Rte. 233. Turn left at (6). The first two miles are very level. A long, gradual ascent begins after you turn right at (7). The road reaches its crest just east of (8). The descent is again long and gradual, making especially excellent terrain for beginning cross-country skiers.

Bikers and skiers may prefer to travel in the opposite direction to take advantage of the relatively gentle rise along the west side of the lake rather than trying to negotiate the steeper climb from (7) to (8).

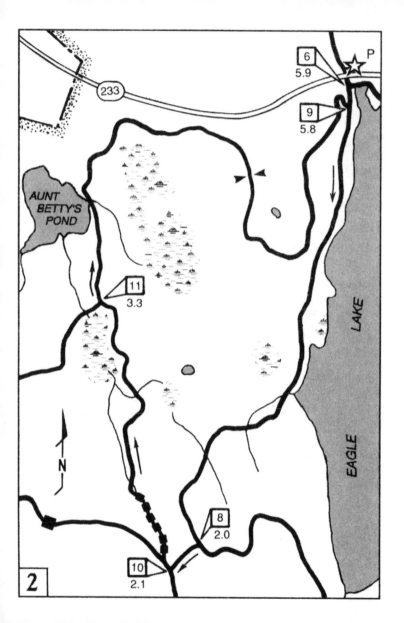

2

Aunt Betty's Pond Loop

Aunt Betty's Pond Loop is unique not only for its unusual place names but also because the pond is the largest on Mt. Desert Island to which there is not vehicle access. If you see a canoe on this pond, it's been carried in.

After parking your car in the Eagle Lake parking lot about three miles west of Bar Harbor on Rte. 233, walk west along the footpath to where you can turn left. Go under Rte. 233, and at [6] continue straight along the west side of Eagle Lake. The first mile is flat, but the second climbs to 468 feet at [8]. Turn right here. At [10] the carriage roads intersect in a K shape. Stay to the right.

If you're skiing, the fun starts now. The carriage road twists and turns as it drops steeply, crossing a meandering stream over six little bridges. The crossings are known as Seven Bridges. Old-timers say the "seven bridges" actually include a culvert below the six structures.

The long descent ends near Gilmore Meadow, which you'll see on your left. Stay to the right at [11]. Aunt Betty's Pond, shallow and marshy, appears on the left. Exactly who Aunt Betty was is still unclear to historians. The name can be found on maps dating back to 1890.

Leaving the pond, the carriage road rises from the marshy lowlands to an elevation where the views of the pond and of Eagle Lake and Cadillac Mountain are magnificent. At [9] turn left to return to your car.

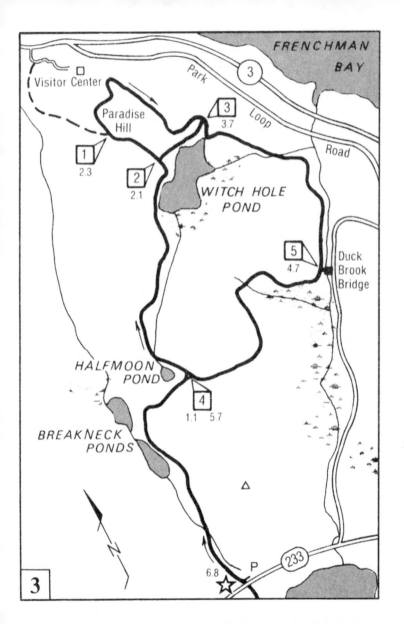

FRENCHMAN BAY

Visitor Center

Paradise Hill

Park Loop Road

③ 3.7

Witch Hole Pond

① 2.3

② 2.1

⑤ 4.7 — Duck Brook Bridge

HALFMOON POND

④ 1.1 5.7

BREAKNECK PONDS

N

233

6.8 P ☆

3

3

Witch Hole Pond Loop

The Witch Hole Pond Loop can be reached from three points. This map shows access from the Eagle Lake parking lot three miles west of Bar Harbor on Rte. 233.

In addition, however, you can park at the Acadia National Park Visitor Center in Hulls Cove and walk the one-half-mile path where it joins the Paradise Hill portion of the loop.

You can also drive to the Duck Brook Bridge by proceeding 2.5 miles west of Bar Harbor on Rte. 233 and turning north on an unmarked road. Go one mile and park just beyond the only building on your left. Cross the bridge on foot. The carriage road skirts Duck Brook Bridge at that point.

The Witch Hole Pond Loop is surfaced with fine gravel and maintained especially for bicycles, wheelchairs, and strollers. Horses are not allowed.

From the Eagle Lake parking lot, walk west along the foot-path to the carriage road. Turn right. This section of the carriage road is level and passes the Breakneck Ponds. At [4] turn left and continue for one mile where you'll see Witch Hole Pond on your right. A left turn at [2] will take you up Paradise Hill for a fantastic view of Hulls Cove and Frenchman Bay. Be sure to keep to the right at [1]. Turn left at [3], and a mile farther, at [5], you'll see a spectacular triple-arched bridge on your left rising 40 feet over Duck Brook.

For a shorter trip, park at Duck Brook Bridge and follow the 3.3-mile loop around Witch Hole Pond only, taking the .2-mile connection between [2] and [3]. Witch Hole Pond and Paradise Hill loops together combine to make a 4.6-mile trip.

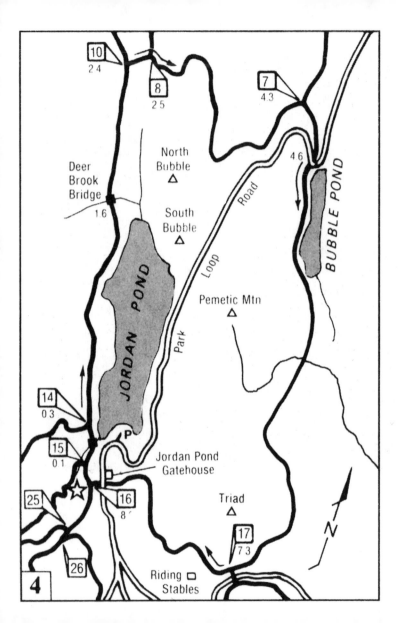

4

Jordan-Bubble Ponds Loop

An ideal excursion to begin in the early morning is the Jordan-Bubble Ponds Loop. Sargent and Penobscot mountains rise to the west, shading both ponds in the afternoon, but the morning sun shines brilliantly on Jordan Pond.

Park in the Jordan Pond parking lot, .2 mile north of the Jordan Pond Tea House. Walk south along the Park Loop Road to the Jordan Pond Gate (across the road from the stone Jordan Pond Gatehouse). Starting here, turn right at [16] and continue north.

The carriage road rises to lovely vistas overlooking Jordan Pond as it cuts across a large rock slide south of Deer Brook Bridge. Turn right at intersections [10] and [8]. An elevation drop of 168 feet begins at [8]. Turn right again at [7]. Shortly thereafter the carriage road crosses the Park Loop Road and then borders Bubble Pond for its entire length.

An early start on this loop should have put you near the shore of Bubble Pond near lunchtime. Here picnic tables or a shoreline

boulder provide delightful spots to rest and snack.

In the latter part of the day you will be in the shadows of Pemetic Mountain and the Triad as you follow the carriage road south. It winds past [17] and the Wildwood Stables back to Jordan Pond Gate, completing 8.6 miles.

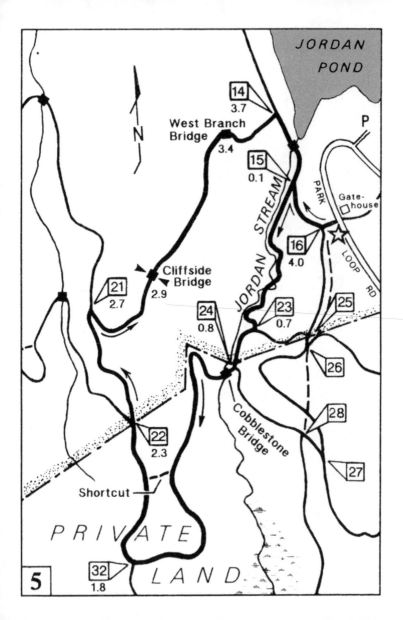

5

Jordan Stream Loop

One of the prettiest and most exciting cross-country-ski runs on the carriage roads follows the descent of Jordan Stream from the Jordan Pond Tea House to the Cobblestone Bridge.

Park at the Jordan Pond parking lot, .2 mile north of the Jordan Pond Tea House. Walk south along the Park Loop Road to the Jordan Pond Gate (across the road from the stone Jordan Pond Gatehouse).

Starting here, turn right at [16]. Take a left at [15]. The downhill run follows the curves of the gurgling stream at a fairly steep descent. Turn right at [23] and at [24].

At this point you have crossed the park boundary onto private land that is open to the public. Please stay on the carriage roads. These roads are sometimes plowed in the winter.

Here Jordan Stream runs under the Cobblestone Bridge, unique in that it is the only carriage road bridge built of cobbles (stream-rounded stones).

One-half mile beyond the bridge, a shortcut has been cut to the right. There is no intersection sign at this junction. The shortcut cuts off about three-quarters of a mile. Turn right at [32] if you do not take the shortcut. If you do take the shortcut, turn right where you rejoin the carriage road, and at [22] as you re-enter the park. Another right at [21] leads you to the Cliffside Bridge, where a wonderful view of the Jordan Pond House (to the left) and Little Long Pond (to the right) reward your steep climb. The road continues over West Branch Bridge to [14], where an additional right turn eventually brings you back to your starting point.

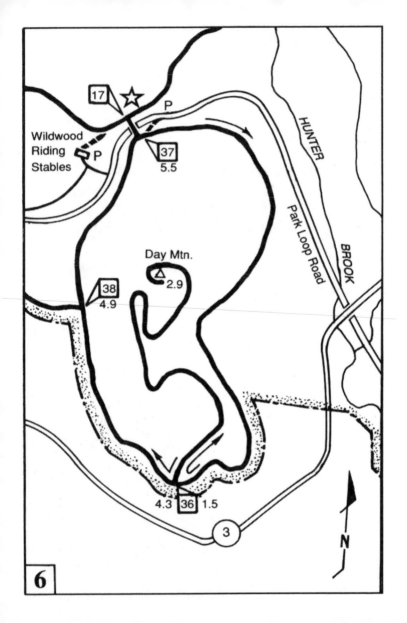

6

Day Mountain Loop

Slightly over a mile from the ocean, the 583-foot, softly rounded peak of Day Mountain rises. A carriage road goes right to the top.

To begin the Day Mountain Loop, you can park in the right-hand lane of the Park Loop Road near where it passes under the carriage road bridge. A connecting path (dashed line on map) takes you up the bank to the carriage road.

Or you can park at Wildwood Riding Stables. Walk up the trail from behind the stables to intersection [17] and cross the bridge.

At [37] turn left to go around the east side of Day Mountain. At [36] turn right to take the 1.4-mile spur to the top of the mountain. The view from the peak is of the Cranberry Isles and the waters around Northeast Harbor and Southwest Harbor.

Returning to [36], turn right. The carriage road, skirting the west side of the mountain, drops to an intersection, [38], with a connecting carriage road.*

Continue straight. The road rises again to take you back to [37].

In the summer, Day Mountain's proximity to the stables makes it a popular route for horseback riders. This trip can be rough and dusty for walkers.

*Another way to reach the Day Mountain Loop is on this .4-mile connecting carriage road. To find it, drive about .3 mile north of Seal Harbor on Rte. 3. Jordan Pond Road forks off to the left. Take the Jordan Pond Road and watch for a granite bridge about .6 mile farther. The connecting carriage road goes under the road at the bridge and connects with the loop around Day Mountain.

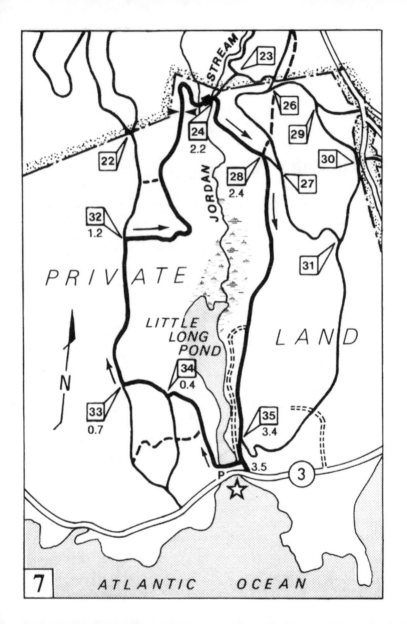

7

Little Long Pond Loop

One of the most popular carriage road loops is the one around Little Long Pond. Easily accessible from Rte. 3 between Seal Harbor and Northeast Harbor, the loop starts at the south end of the pond, where it empties into Bracy Cove. The small parking area is along the road. This entire loop is on private land. It is open to the public, but bicycles are not permitted.

Starting clockwise around the loop, follow the carriage road as it crosses the small dam at the foot of the pond. The terrain gains in elevation as you proceed toward intersections [34] and [33]. Continuing to climb, the half-mile stretch between posts [33] and [32] takes you up and over a hill. Turn right at intersection [32]. About a quarter of a mile farther, where the road curves sharply to the left, there is a good view of the pond and the private boathouse on the far shore. As you continue on, keep to the right to avoid taking the horse trail shortcut, which would steer you away from the Little Long Pond Loop.

After skirting the shoulder of Mitchell Hill, you will cross Cobblestone Bridge, an especially picturesque bridge and the only one in the system made of cobblestones. Again, keep to your right at post [24]. In the winter the trails in this area, if snow-covered, are often groomed for cross-country skiing.

From post [28] south to post [35], fields luxuriant with green grass roll down to the swampy headwaters of the pond in summer. In winter, the gentle slopes are wonderful for skiing and sledding.

When you reach intersection [35] you are nearly back where you started, and you will have completed 3.5 miles.

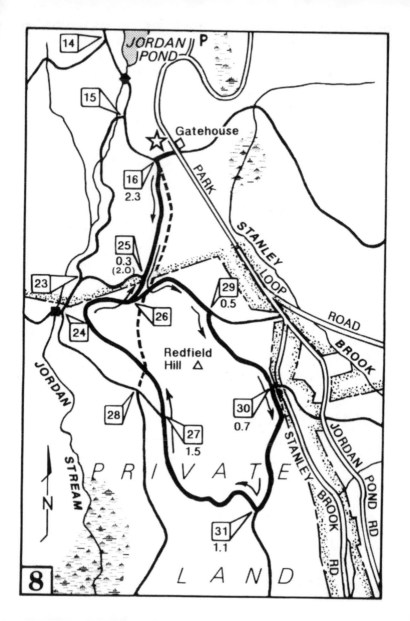

8

Redfield Hill Loop

One of the shortest (2.3 miles) and most easily accessible loops shown in this book is the Redfield Hill Loop. Park at the Jordan Pond parking lot, .2 mile north of the Jordan Pond Tea House. Walk south along the Park Loop Road to the Jordan Pond Gate (across the road from the stone Jordan Pond Gatehouse).

Starting here, turn left at [16]. Follow the carriage road south past [25], where you will cross the park boundary onto private land that is open to the public. Please stay on the carriage roads in this area. These roads are sometimes plowed in the winter.

Turn left at [26]. Just east of [26] a horse path crosses the carriage road. It looks much like a carriage road and is shown on the map as a dashed line. The horse path overlaps the carriage road for a few hundred feet, then exits to the north, paralleling the carriage road from [26] to [16].

Stay to the right at [29], [30], and [31]. You will then descend for .4 mile to [27]. Take the right fork there. One-tenth of a mile past [27] the horse path again crosses the carriage road. Stay to the left, and the carriage road will loop back around to [26]. A left turn at [26] will take you back into the park and direct you to your point of origin.

An even shorter loop (1.2 miles) in this area is to take the stretch from [16] to [25]. Then turn right at [25], [23], and [15]. From [23] to [15] the carriage road climbs as it parallels the bank of the meandering Jordan Stream.

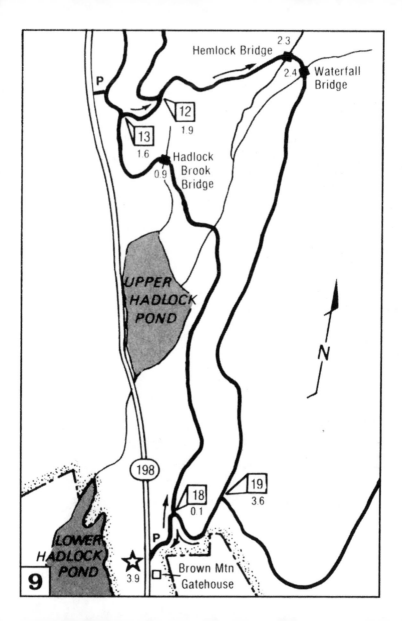

9

Hadlock Brook Loop

Rising to an elevation of 500 feet, the Hadlock Brook Loop is a lovely 3.9-mile circuit that offers something for everyone — level, gently rising, and steep grades, a pond, a waterfall, and wonderful views.

A mile north of Northeast Harbor on Rte. 198 is the stone Brown Mountain Gatehouse. Park in the lot just north of that. A short rise leads to intersection [18], where you will turn left. The carriage road continues straight and level for over a mile. It skirts Upper Hadlock Pond, where loons can sometimes be heard calling in the early mornings. Two right turns at [13] and [12] lead up to one of the steepest carriage road grades in the system. But you will be amply rewarded for efforts; awaiting you at the top is the highest waterfall in Acadia National Park and two of Rockefeller's loveliest bridges, Hemlock and Waterfall.

Hadlock Brook drops 40 feet and then cascades under

Waterfall Bridge into a deep ravine before finally emptying into Upper Hadlock Pond.

The descent from the bridges to [19] is a gradual one, offering wonderful views of Hadlock Pond and the surrounding forests. Turn right at [19] and left at [18] to return to your car. If you prefer a gentle climb, reverse your direction for an easy ascent up and fast trip down, finishing with the level path along Upper Hadlock Pond.

This loop can also be reached from the Parkman Mountain parking lot one-half mile north of Upper Hadlock Pond on Rte. 198.

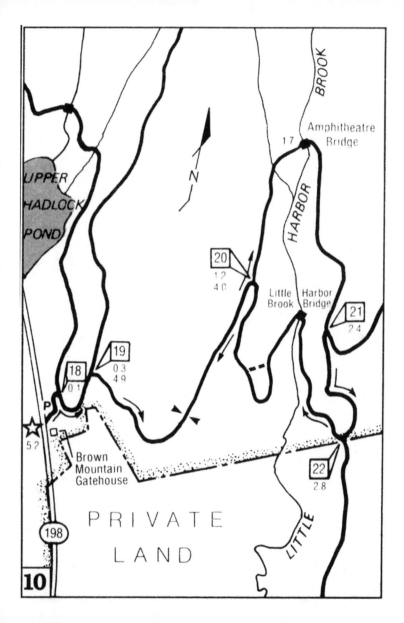

UPPER
HADLOCK
POND

BROOK

Amphitheatre
Bridge
17

HARBOR

20
1 2
4 0

Little
Brook

Harbor
Bridge

21
2 4

19
0 3
4 9

18
0 1

P

52

Brown
Mountain
Gatehouse

22
2 8

198

PRIVATE

LAND

LITTLE

N

10

10

Ampitheatre Loop

The Ampitheatre Loop takes you deep into the heart of Acadia National Park, where the sounds of traffic and civilization fade away.

Park in the lot just north of the Brown Mountain Gatehouse, one mile north of Northeast Harbor on Rte. 198. The carriage road leads up a short hill to intersection [18], where you will turn right and again right at [19]. A left turn at [20] takes you along the western rim of a box canyon that terminates at Amphitheatre Bridge — at 236 feet, the longest of the Rockefeller bridges. Strong winds sweep the route between the bridge and [21] in the winter, often making this stretch nearly bare of snow and extremely cold. Stay to the right at [21] and [22]. You will lose elevation, dropping to the lowest point at the Little Harbor Brook Bridge.

From the bridge to [20] you will climb once more. Horseback riders and hikers have cut a shortcut through the woods about

halfway along this stretch. If you take the shortcut you'll save about .2 mile but will miss some excellent views of the harbor and islands.

Retrace your steps from [20] back to the gate, but don't fail to pause at the vistas to enjoy the sight of the Cranberry Isles and the sailboats in the Western Way.

This loop can also be reached from the east. From the Jordan Pond gate turn left at either [14] or [15]. See the Jordan Stream Loop map.

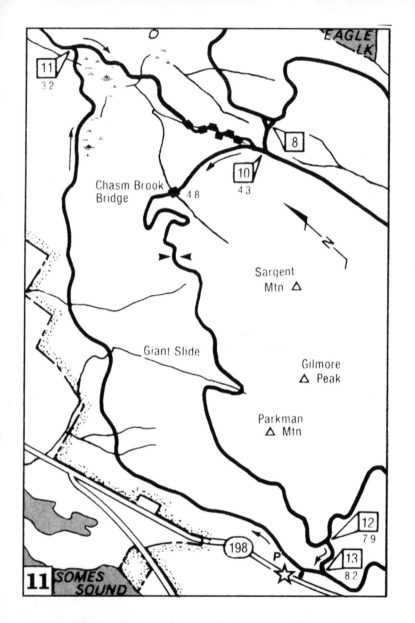

EAGLE LK

11
3.2

8

10
4.3

Chasm Brook
Bridge

4.8

Sargent
Mtn △

Giant Slide

Gilmore
△ Peak

Parkman
△ Mtn

198

P

12
7.9

13
8.2

11 SOMES
SOUND

11

Giant Slide Loop

The Giant Slide Loop takes the hiker or skier higher than any other carriage road, climbing up the shoulder of Sargent Mountain to an elevation of 780 feet.

This loop starts at the Parkman Mountain parking lot on Rte. 198, one-half mile north of Upper Hadlock Pond. Follow the spur trail to the carriage road for 100 feet. Turn left onto the carriage road and settle down for a long (3.2-mile), leisurely, level stretch. During the autumn the deciduous trees in this area are in full color.

At [11] turn right and proceed south, where you will cross six little bridges* that span a meandering stream. A sharp right at [10] continues the ascent up the side of Sargent Mountain. At Chasm Brook Bridge the stream takes a sudden plunge of 15 feet in full view of anyone stopping to take a moment's breather after an arduous ascent. Climbing still higher, you can look down on the carriage roads you were on moments earlier.

Before beginning a steep descent, pause to enjoy unparalleled views of Somes Sound to the west.

Turn right at [12] and again at [13]. You have traveled 8.2 miles.

*See Aunt Betty's Pond Loop, page 19, for information on the six bridges.

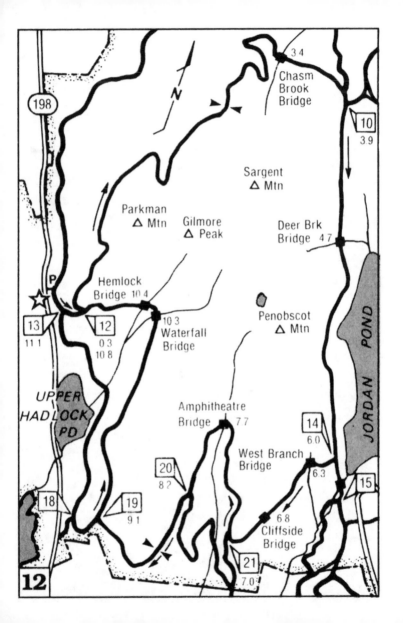

198

Chasm
Brook
Bridge   3 4

10
3.9

Sargent
△ Mtn

Parkman
△ Mtn   Gilmore
△ Peak

Deer Brk
Bridge   4 7

P

Hemlock
Bridge 10 4

13
11 1

12
0 3
10 8

10 3
Waterfall
Bridge

Penobscot
△ Mtn

JORDAN POND

UPPER
HADLOCK
PD

Amphitheatre
Bridge   7 7

14
6.0

West Branch
Bridge

20
8 2

6.3

18

19
9 1

15

6 8
Cliffside
Bridge

21
7.0

12

12

Around Mountain Loop

The longest trip in the carriage road system, the Around Mountain Loop, covers roads that are shown in this book as segments of other loops. The "mountain" you are going around is actually several mountains. Sargent, Parkman, and Penobscot are the major peaks surrounded by this 11.1-mile circuit.

This trip starts at the Parkman Mountain parking lot one-half mile north of Hadlock Pond on Rte. 198.

Details of particular stretches of this trip can be found by reading the descriptions (going clockwise) of the Giant Slide, Jordan-Bubble Ponds, Jordan Stream, Amphitheatre, and Hadlock loops.

History
by Andrew Vietze

Young John D. Rockefeller, Jr. first visited Mt. Desert in 1893 while he was a student. Rockefeller was evidently quite taken with the place because in 1908 he decided to return with his family. His wife, Abby, was pregnant with their third child, and her physician summered in Blue Hill. The family moved up to Bar Harbor for the summer to be near him, and he delivered a boy, Nelson, on August 8.

The Rockefellers loved the island, and soon bought a home on a 150-acre plot on Barr Hill, overlooking Seal Harbor's Eastern Way. The Rockefellers called their Tudor-style cottage the Eyrie, and they greatly expanded the place, adding huge new wings and dozens of dormers, until it was a massive hundred-room mansion.

Rockefeller's life in New York was anything but quiet and peaceful, and one of the greatest appeals of the Eyrie was the ability for JDR to get away from the noise and drama of the city — and its automobiles. He enjoyed the fact that cars were not allowed on Mt. Desert Island, the result of a huge battle that had been waged two years prior that pitted locals, who wanted cars, against the rusticators, who had been moving up in droves since the 1880s. A ban was passed in 1908. It would prove to be short-lived.

At about the same time, another gas-guzzling machine had the wealthy folks in a state of alarm — the portable sawmill. The new gas-powered saws gave loggers more mobility than previous steam- and water-powered devices. Large tracts of woodlands on the island were owned by timber companies, and they were beginning to fell trees.

Several summer residents — with Bostonians George B. Dorr and Charles Eliot at the forefront — banded together in opposition to this threat and the seeds of the first national park east of the Mississippi were planted. The pair's nascent organization quickly began acquiring significant pieces of land all across the island. In September of 1914, George Dorr wrote to John D. Rockefeller, Jr. In the note he asked JDR for his help "protecting and developing to public use the natural beauty of the island and promoting its welfare as a resort home." History has lost Rockefeller's response, but he and Dorr struck up an agreement and began working together.

Rockefeller inherited more than a fortune from his father, he also shared his love of the outdoors. When he was still a young boy, his father, "Senior," began building a network of gravel roads on their Forest Hills estate in Cleveland Heights, Ohio. An expanse of more than six hundred acres outside the city, it sprawled across hills and dales, and the young Junior loved to explore its woods and lakeshores and especially to ride alongside his father in horse-drawn carriages.

All of Junior's interests seemed to find a home on Mt.Desert. He loved the quietude and the privacy — Mainers tended to leave him alone — and he could tool around behind his carriage without worrying about being hit by a car. After moving to Seal Harbor, Rockefeller purchased the land surrounding his property when it came available, and soon he added more and more acreage — Long Pond, the south end of Jordan Pond, a parcel along Otter Cove, the eastern shore of Bubble Pond, the north shore of Eagle Lake, a swath encircling Upper Hadlock Pond, and another around Witch Hole Pond and Aunt Betty Pond.

Rockefeller had already begun conceptualizing a system of carriage roads on the properties he owned, much like the one his father had built in Ohio. He saw a network of crushed-rock lanes as an ideal way to open the interior of the island — Jordan Pond, Eagle Lake, the small water bodies, and the valleys between the peaks — not only to horse carriages but also to hikers. His vision was to connect Frenchman Bay up north with the sea to the south, making it possible to wend one's way through the park without ever having to get into a car.

The shovels first hit dirt in 1911 on JDR's own Seal Harbor property. He purchased a parcel of land west of Long Pond and another that reached all the way up to the shore of Jordan Pond. Roads began to thread through them, and JDR wanted to link them all. But to do so he would have to cross land owned by the Hancock trustees, the organization headed by Dorr, that was setting aside land on the island for conservation. Rockefeller asked if he could build a right of way and was granted permission to do so. He could construct roads on reservation land, as it was called, at his own expense, but he had no legal right to the byway or the acreage it crossed. That was good enough for Rockefeller. By 1915, the trustees passed a resolution formalizing the agreement, and JDR's contractors started felling trees, filling holes, laying down roadbeds, lining the sixteen-foot lanes with coping stones, and ultimately surfacing them with gravel.

Rockefeller was quick to locate talent in the area. By 1916 he was working with Charles Simpson, an engineer from Sullivan who had done projects for the Kebo Valley Golf Club, the

Town of Northeast Harbor, and for landscape architect Joseph Curtis. The pair worked together for six years, a period that saw roads built in the area between Seal Harbor and Jordan Pond. When Simpson retired, JDR hired his son, Paul, who worked as chief engineer until the last carriage road was built in 1940.

The public looked on with interest as Rockefeller's roads became longer and longer. During all of the construction, JDR was a frequent visitor to work sites. He'd talk to foremen, make sure views were being highlighted, check gradients, see to it that the roads were three layers, with a six- or eight-inch crown for good drainage. In other words, state of the art.

In 1919, the year Lafayette National Park (it was renamed as Acadia in 1929) was dedicated, crews came across a problem in the building of a road near Jordan Stream. The fix? A bridge. JDR hired architect Welles Bosworth to build the first significant span on the carriage roads, known as the Cobblestone Bridge. With a long curve and parapets overlooking the stream, it's the perfect complement to the carriage road that leads to it and a marvel of engineering. Over the years, fifteen more bridges would follow, each prettier than the next, looking like something out of a storybook.

Not everyone was happy with all the construction going

on, however. In August of 1919, Rockefeller received a letter from George Wharton Pepper, a Philadelphia lawyer, summer resident of Northeast Harbor, and future senator. Pepper had heard that Rockefeller was eyeing a section of hills and forest between Jordan Pond and the Hadlock ponds, known as the Amphitheatre, and he didn't like it. He thought extending the carriage roads into the area — his home was nearby — was "a serious mistake." "The Amphitheatre is an as yet unbroken forest," he wrote. "Pierce this with a road or roads and its character will vanish."

The balance between wildness and accessibility is a delicate one in any park, and Pepper and many others believed that with more roads "the park will be overdeveloped and due proportion of wilderness destroyed." The controversy brought construction to a halt, and it highlighted a conflict that had always been in place between Rockefeller and George Dorr.

While Dorr was bold and perhaps even a little reckless, Rockefeller was serious and thoughtful, and their views on preservation were somewhat at odds. Both wanted to save the lands of Mt. Desert in perpetuity — and for public use — but they came at conservation from different schools. Dorr was a wilderness advocate who believed in preserving large chunks of land for the sake of it and having the least impact possible.

Rockefeller, on the other hand, believed nature's beauty had to be made accessible.

"He was the part of the school of thought that man could enhance nature," says Acadia interpretive ranger Betty Lyle, who runs a program on the carriage roads each summer.

The opposing rusticators were not only disturbed by the opening of the wild fastness and the building of roads into this stunning natural bowl but also by what they anticipated would happen next. "A lot of people were afraid the roads would eventually be opened to cars," explains Lyle, adding that construction was halted for about ten years. "A lot of them came up for the peace and quiet."

Much as Rockefeller — and many island residents — hated it, cars were coming. In 1913 the ban on automobiles on Mt. Desert had been eased, allowing them on the Bar Harbor side of the island. Two years later, however, all restrictions were removed, and drivers could go wherever they pleased. This most certainly spurred Rockefeller into action.

He was so opposed to keeping cars out of the interior of the park and off his carriage roads that he volunteered to finance, design, and help build the Park Loop Road, the twenty-seven-mile highway that links many of Acadia's biggest attractions. He figured it was inevitable that cars would make their way into the park's heart, and he wanted it done in a way he could control. "I would not have been interested to build any roads had I thought they would ever be made available for automobiles," he wrote in a letter.

Carriage-road construction continued until 1940, until Rockefeller reached the end of what he wanted done. All told the roads cross forty-five miles, passing dozens of peaks and ponds and lakes, and rolling over sixteen historic bridges. Landscaping around many sections was done by famed architect Beatrix Farrand, who began working on a garden for the Rockefellers in the early twenties and moved to the roads next, and the system was lauded by the even more famous Frederick Law Olmsted, who had designed Central Park.

After paying the roads a visit in 1932, Olmsted wrote to Rockefeller: "Driving in horse-drawn vehicles along narrow, winding woodland roads amid beautiful and varied scenery, completely free from the annoyance, and even the dread of meeting motor cars, is so real and extraordinarily rare today that systematic provision for it may reasonably be expected to develop into one of the most unique attractions of the park and the island."

John D. Rockefeller, Jr. would gift this unique attraction to the park — and all the land upon which they sat. When added up, the sum of his donation is astounding. "He gave the park about a third of all its acreage," says Ranger Lyle.

Until he died in 1960, JDR paid for the maintenance of the carriage roads. When he passed away, care of "Mr. Rockefeller's Roads" reverted to the National Park Service. "They went from having a sixty-person crew [looking after them] to a two-person crew," says Lyle.

By the 1980s, when mountain bikers discovered the roads en masse, several miles had fallen into disrepair. News stories came out lamenting the state of the roads, 25 percent of which were so overgrown they were half as wide as when they were built.

As they did when the park was born, generous summer people offered their help, again with a Rockefeller at the fore. John D. Rockefeller, Jr.'s son, David, along with the Friends of Acadia, began a project to create an endowment for the beloved icons, matching federal funds to the tune of $4 million. Construction lasted until the 1990s. The bridges were next. In the early 2000s, the park service had most of them repointed.

Today, the days of controversy are long gone and the venerable byways are in great shape — they're considered the finest example of broken-stone roads in the country — and are used by cyclists, walkers, hikers, horses, and photographers. Just as

Rockefeller had planned, they connect many of the park's most beautiful places. They link the north to the south, making it possible to travel the entire park without ever having to sit in the confines of a car.

And, as Rockefeller might have loved most of all, horse and carriage rides are available on them all summer long.

Distance Index to Carriage Roads Loops

(in order of increasing distance, listing maximum change in elevation)

Distance (in miles)	Elevation Change (in feet)	Loop
1.2	140	Gatehouse to Jordan Stream and back
2.3	200	Redfield Hill
2.7	120	Day Mountain (excluding spur to top)
3.3	80	Witch Hole Pond (from Duck Brook Bridge)
3.5	160	Little Long Pond
3.9	280	Hadlock Brook
4.0	280	Jordan Stream
4.6	80	Witch Hole Pond and Paradise Hill (from Duck Brook Bridge)
5.2	200	Amphitheatre
5.5	400	Day Mountain (including spur to top)
5.8	200	Eagle Lake
5.9	200	Aunt Betty Pond
6.8	100	Witch Hole Pond and Paradise Hill (from Rte. 233)
8.2	560	Giant Slide
8.6	200	Jordan-Bubble Ponds
11.1	480	Around Mountain